Lewis and Clark

VOYAGE OF DISCOVERY™
The Story Behind the Scenery ®

PHOTOGRAPHY BY **David Muench** • TEXT BY **Dan Murphy**

DAVID MUENCH, leading landscape photographer, brings to these pages a keen sensitivity to nature and an artist's instinct for mood and lighting. Commissioned by the National Park Service to commemorate photographically the epic journey of Lewis and Clark, Dave spent nearly a year in this pursuit. The resulting photo-murals, presented here, are on permanent display at the Museum of Westward Expansion in St. Louis.

DAN MURPHY, in his perceptive, unpretentious text, reveals a compassionate regard for the rugged yet intensely human members of the Lewis and Clark Expedition. Dan, a career employee of the National Park Service and first supervisor for the museum, became personally caught up in the drama of the Lewis and Clark journals while serving at Jefferson National Expansion Memorial during the installation of the photo-murals.

JEFFERSON NATIONAL EXPANSION MEMORIAL is administered by the National Park Service in St. Louis, Missouri, for two centuries the "Gateway to the West." There the soaring, 630-foot Gateway Arch honors those who pioneered the West; the immense Museum of Westward Expansion tells their story. The photo-murals with which this book is concerned are a major feature of the museum, magnificently displayed in a 16-foot-high exhibit extending 500 feet along one wall of the museum.

Cover Photo: Salmon River, Idaho. Page 1: Gateway Arch Photo by Joe Matthews.

Book design by K.C. DenDooven.

Seventh Printing, 1999

LEWIS AND CLARK: VOYAGE OF DISCOVERY. © 1977 KC PUBLICATIONS, INC.
*"The Story Behind the Scenery"; "in pictures... The Continuing Story"; the parallelogram forms
and colors within are registered in the U.S. Patent and Trademark Office.*
LC 76-57451. ISBN 0-916122-50-6.

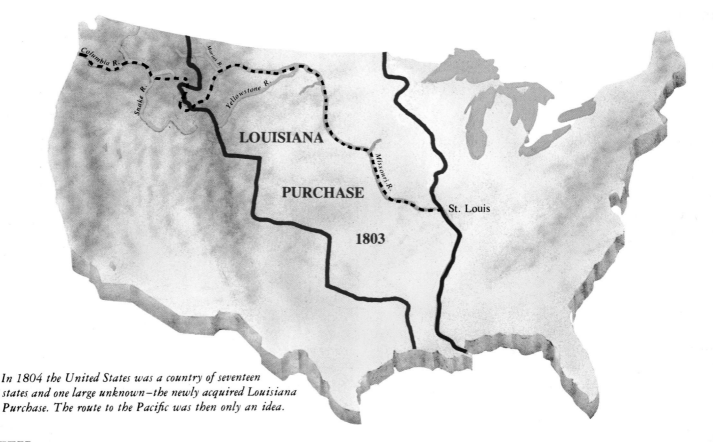

Columbia R.

Maria's R.

Snake R.

Yellowstone R.

LOUISIANA

PURCHASE

Missouri R.

St. Louis

1803

In 1804 the United States was a country of seventeen states and one large unknown—the newly acquired Louisiana Purchase. The route to the Pacific was then only an idea.

When Thomas Jefferson was elected president of the United States of America, he chose as his private secretary a man whose qualifications for that job were dubious, and whose spelling, at best, was imaginative. Yet it was an excellent choice. To understand why, we must go back to those tumultuous years when the American Revolution was just over, when wounds received at Lexington and Yorktown still ached on humid days. The treaty ending the war had given the new country the land clear to the Mississippi River. Most of the population was still along the eastern seaboard, but the astonishing story of America's westward expansion had already begun. Hunters and trappers, then land speculators, were crossing the Appalachians. Woods that had been silent since the ice ages suddenly heard the "whack" of iron axes. Through Kentucky and Tennessee and Indiana the frontiersmen spread, and now and then the woods even heard the sounds of families and babies.

The other side of the Mississippi, the west side, was claimed by Spain—a fact that didn't mean very much in the wilderness—and a few men built rafts and crossed over. Spain's world empire was on the decline, and there is abundant evidence that already President Jefferson was planning for the day when the United States would move its boundary across the Mississippi. Her self-motivated pioneers were already there.

If (for Jefferson, *when*) the nation did come to include the West, what in fact would she have? Nobody even knew how far the West extended, let alone what was included. It would have to be explored and mapped. No country can govern what it doesn't even know.

There was another motivation for exploration in the West—the old dream of a water route to India. That was, after all, what Columbus had been after when he discovered the New World, a distraction that was proving to be a longer interruption (and a richer prize) than anyone had expected. But the dream was not dead. Waterborne commerce between the Orient and Europe or even the eastern United States meant certain wealth. Jefferson knew that a major river called the "Missouri" poured into the Mississippi from the west; he also knew that a sea captain named Gray had found a major river emptying into the Pacific and named it the "Columbia." Could it be that their headwaters interlocked? There was no evidence for this, but some men thought it to be so. They said a crew could take a boat up the Missouri to its source, do a one-day portage, and float down the Columbia to the Pacific—and Cathay! It had to be checked out.

Add one more fact and the puzzle of the secretary who could not spell is almost clear: That fact is the consuming curiosity of Thomas Jefferson. He was a good lawyer, a skilled politician, and would prove a consummate diplomat; but he was also an astronomer, an archeologist, an inventor, and above all a naturalist. All the questions about the phenomena of nature fascinated him: when various flowers bloomed, what fossils revealed, how animals lived, what plants were edible. The West held the lure of infinite discovery.

For all these reasons, Jefferson had long been interested in sending an expedition into the West. He had already been involved with some preliminary attempts that had failed. Now he was president, and the time was almost ripe. So he chose as his private secretary Meriwether Lewis. Lewis was a Virginia neighbor of Jefferson,

I Set out at 4 o'Clock P.M., in the presence of many of the neighbouring inhabitents, and proceeded on under a jentle brease up the Missourie. . . .

WILLIAM CLARK

accustomed to outdoor life. He had served with distinction in the frontier army, where he had shown intelligence, good judgment, and the ability to lead men. He was just the man to head Jefferson's expedition. Much of their association in the yet-unfinished White House was spent in planning that journey—in trying to foresee the unforeseeable. Jefferson also arranged "cram" courses for Lewis in navigation, medicine, and natural history.

Suddenly the orderly process was interrupted with news that came like a thunderbolt from the storm that was raging in France. Napoleon Bonaparte, taking a short break from "re-drawing" the map of Europe, had demanded and received the Louisiana Territory from Spain. In this new light the prospect for westward expansion looked different indeed. Now the West, instead of being in the weak grip of a declining empire, was in the hands of an aggressive military genius whose ambition knew no bounds. Not only was westward expansion in question, Jefferson now had to worry about hanging on to the area between the Appalachians and the Mississippi! The area's only outlet to world markets was via the Mississippi and, especially, New Orleans. It was impossible to countenance a foreign power in control of that outlet, especially an aggressive one.

It was not an idle threat. Word reached Jefferson that Napoleon had already sent an army to establish a base of operations in the Caribbean islands, and was preparing another to strengthen Louisiana. Jefferson responded with the two faces of diplomacy. He let it be known that the U.S. would ally itself with England and fight France if necessary, and at the same time he sent emissaries to Paris to try to buy New Orleans. The story of how they came back with *all* of the Louisiana Territory—that is, all of the land drained by the Mississippi and its tributaries, clear to the Rocky Mountains—is fascinating but must be told briefly: Napoleon's Caribbean army was wiped out—by yellow fever and by a brilliant black general named Toussaint L'Overture. Napoleon realized two things: that he probably could not hold New Orleans against England's sea power and that the filtering into the West of America's seemingly self-propelled pioneers could not be stopped. He decided to make the best of it and sell the whole area to the United States, thereby gathering gold for further European adventures. Jefferson's expedition to the West was now a certainty, and he wrote out the official instruction for the "Corps of Discovery." It is long and covers such matters as recruiting and discharging men, the route to be taken, dealings with Indians, and observation of natural history. The crux, though, is this paragraph:

The object of your mission is to explore the Missouri River, and such principal stream [sic] of it, as, by its course and communication with the water of the Pacific Ocean may offer the most direct and practicable water communication across this continent for the purposes of commerce.

Jefferson asked Lewis to choose a co-captain, and Lewis chose William Clark. They had served together in the army. Clark was a psychological complement to Lewis. He was plain and hearty where Lewis was sometimes withdrawn and introspective, bluff and cheery where Lewis might be intellectual. Like Lewis, he was experienced in wilderness travel and was gifted as a leader. And he would prove to be superb at dealing with Indians.

The winter of 1803–04 found the captains at a place they called Camp Wood, on the Mississippi across from the mouth of the Missouri. It was a time of preparation. They had chosen some men already, but experienced St. Louis traders convinced them they needed more. Volunteers came in; they selected some, rejected others. Gradually they gathered a crew of experienced frontiersmen, superb in dealing with hardship or emergency but the very devil to discipline or organize. Names that would become legend later, like Colter and Droulliard, first show up in disciplinary reports for drinking or staying away late or arguing with officers. But they were good men.

The expedition had been issued supplies from the army supply depot at Harpers Ferry, such as gunpowder packed in lead cannisters that could themselves be melted into bullets. Now they gathered Indian trade goods: fourteen bales of beads and tobacco and ribbon and fishhooks. Foodstuffs: flour, pork, whiskey (a hundred gallons), salt, corn. Candles. And scientific instruments: sextant and thermometer, telescope and quadrant, and the all-important notebooks (blank now; who could guess what would fill those pages?). They gathered medical texts and instruments; in the wilderness they must become self-sufficient.

Finally, the end of the waiting was in sight. They could tell the winter was passing, as the problem of mud replaced the problem of snow, and one day they saw a few white trilliums blooming in the Illinois woods. The rush of last-minute details began, and there was the nervous excitement that preludes any voyage, let alone one like this. They knew they were almost ready when Captain Clark ordered the boat into the river to see if the load was distributed properly. (It wasn't.) One week later they went to bed under skies threatening rain. But this was to be their last sleep in Camp Wood; Captain Clark had told them they would leave the next day.

Overleaf: Wood (DuBois) River

*This being my birth day I order'd a Saddle of fat vennison, an Elk fleece &
a Bevartail to be cooked and a Desert of Cheries, Plumbs, Raspberres currents and
grapes. . . . the Praries Contain Cheres, Apple, Grapes, Currents, Raspburry,
Goosberry, Hastlenuts and a great vairety of Plants & flours not common to the US.*

WILLIAM CLARK

On August 1, 1804, the expedition stayed in camp, waiting for some Oto Indians to come in for the expedition's first full-fledged council (part of the diplomatic work President Jefferson had assigned them). They called this spot "Council Bluffs," as we do now (though the river has since reshaped the area).

The respite was welcome. It was two and a half months upstream since they had pushed off into the Missouri's muddy current. Some books about the expedition skip this period almost entirely, since it deals with things known and familiar—not the total unknown that came later, but the daily journal entries record incidents that would be high drama in any normal context. And they reveal a troop of men beginning to find themselves, developing the self-reliance and internal cohesion that would take this Corps of Discovery across a continent.

They fought the river. Floundering in treacherous sand and mud or frantically pushing off snags, they inched upstream. One man "got snakebit." Captain Lewis bled him, applied a poultice of bark and niter, and he recovered. Full summer on the Missouri meant sudden fierce storms that drenched men and cargo. It meant days of muggy heat, an oven at noon with no breath of breeze. Men suffered sunstroke, rested, and went on. They learned military discipline. One man got fifty lashes for drinking on duty, another a hundred for falling asleep on watch (not cruelty, given their circumstances). And the mosquitoes! "Muskuitors verry troublesom," 'til the men couldn't sleep or even stand still. They smeared themselves with bear grease and went on.

There was horseplay, some of it rough. The journals don't tell much about those times, but it is impossible to imagine a healthy bunch of men, in the boats all day and camped on sandbars all night, without a good deal of shoving, splashing, dunking, and bugs in tin coffee cups.

Confident competence does not need to take itself seriously all of the time. The journals do mention horseplay a few times: once when it develops into a fistfight, and once when some sand gets thrown into York's eyes. But even when there is no mention of it, we can be sure it was there.

The land was good. They ate well, and the hunters daily brought in more game than they could use. They were toiling their way through rich, well-watered bottomlands. And there were some days—red-letter days!—when a south wind let them set the sail and move grandly upstream without the backbreaking work of poling or lining. And always there was a new scene around the next bend.

So this day in camp was a good one for Captain Clark. He was co-leader of an expedition so far successful, and each day he was seeing new things to delight his frontiersman eyes. It was his thirty-fourth birthday.

. . . Serj. Floyd Died with a great deal of Composure, before his death he Said to me, "I am going away" I want you to write me a letter." We buried him on the top of the bluff 1/2 Mile below a Small river to which we Gave his name. . . .

WILLIAM CLARK

Captain Lewis' birthday came along on August 18, and the men made merry. But the next day they were solemn. Sergeant Charles Floyd had become gravely ill. He was a good man, of frontier stock (his father had soldiered with William Clark's famous older brother, George Rogers Clark), and although Floyd had signed on with the present expedition as an enlisted man, his fellow soldiers had elected him sergeant. He had been sick once before, in late July, but had recovered. Now he was down again.

But history could not wait for one man. The captains held a council with the Oto Indians and told them that rivalries among the prairie Indian tribes would have to end, that a new power was now in control of all of them. This must have been startling and even confusing news to the Indians, but they agreed to make peace among themselves, and the captains were pleased.

Sergeant Floyd did not get better. He was in extreme pain, and he couldn't keep either food or medicine down. Captain Clark stayed up with him most of the night, but on the twentieth there was a favorable breeze, so they started under sail. Late in the morning the sick man's pulse went beyond detection. They landed; Charles Floyd whispered, "I'm going away," and died.

Death is always hard to face, but it must have been triply hard for these men in the wilderness far from home. They carried their friend to the top of the highest nearby hill and buried him; Captain Lewis read the service he had hoped he would never have to use on this expedition. The record doesn't tell much about the mood of that day; the journal entry, written in camp that night at the mouth of the newly named Floyd's River, ends simply with, "a butifull evening." It must have been a pensive one.

What must they have thought of the future of the expedition? They were just three months along now, and as yet had encountered no really rough times. But one man had deserted and another had been arrested in the attempt. Now Sergeant Floyd was dead.

Astonishingly, Sergeant Floyd would be the expedition's only death. Today we think he died of appendicitis. The illness he had suffered two weeks earlier was probably from an infected appendix, which later perforated. In those days the condition could not have been treated properly even in New York or London; so even this one death was not directly attributable to the journey.

Before winter another man would be dismissed, the last man to leave the expedition. But things of the future were hidden that night, for the play was still beginning. The sand bar was the stage, the driftwood fire the footlights, the Missouri's murmur the *leit motif,* and the darkness a curtain. The unknown was before them like a blank wall. Their thoughts circled and probed at it, trying to see the other side. Maybe Floyd was there already.

The men elected Patrick Gass to the post left vacant by Sergeant Charles Floyd, U.S.A., and they went on.

Spirit Mound (near Vermillion, South Dakota)

24th AUGUST FRIDAY 1804

*... in an emence Plain a high Hill
is Situated, and appears of a
Conic form, and by the different
nations of Indians in this
quarter is Suppose to be the residence
of Deavels. ... So much do the
Maha, Soues, Ottoes and
other neighbouring nations believe
this fable, that no Consideration
is Suffecient to induce
them to approach the hill.*

WILLIAM CLARK

Life—the process of getting up each day and doing wh
must be done—became a peculiar combination of the f
miliar and the new. The river was an old acquaintan
now. They knew what its temperature would be as th
stepped into it in the morning, how the mud would su
at their boots, and how the pull of the current against t
tow-rope would feel. They knew that the day would g
hot by noon, that the hours of the afternoon would see
interminably long and the evening's rest impossibly d
tant, and that the mosquitoes would not go away.

They hoped the river would some day become
highway of commerce. Now it was their lifeline—den
thickets and cottonwoods meandering across the prair
bearing up their boats, and showing them the route to t
mountains. But the river with its whims and grand ind
ference could also be their undoing. It undercut the s
along the banks and loosened it, so that great stretches
trees and all—would let go all at once and fall into t
river. There were some close calls. If the bank in co
lapsing didn't get a boat and crew, the resulting wa
might! And there were "sawyers"—whole trees bobbi
in the current, sometimes wedged at the bottom of t
river—that threatened to capsize or even demolish a car
less boat.

So carefully, slowly, they toiled up the river. Eve
turn was a new problem of navigation against the curre
and the river's obstacles, but every turn also brought
new vista. And, after they had marveled at each new thir
it was the job of the Corps of Discovery to examine, te
and record it. Captain Clark documented the location
each bend in the river, the kinds of trees, and any ou
crops of fossils. President Jefferson was particularly inte

walked on Shore, . . . Saw
umbers of Buffalow & Goats,
saw a Hare & believe he
un into a hole in the Side of
hill. . . . None of those
Joats has any Beard, they are
ll Keenly made, and is butifull.

WILLIAM CLARK

;ted in the latter: He himself had discovered the giant
round-sloth fossil (now known as *Megalonyx jeffersoni*)
ad kept it in his collection in the East Room of the White
Iouse. That huge animal might—just might—still live in
ie vast country that Lewis and Clark were entering!

The prairies stretched far and changed little. But,
ke any plains watercourse, the river supported a pro-
eration of flora and fauna—life drawn to the river by its
ater, the shelter of its copses, and the enriched environ-
ient. Two days upstream from the bluff where they bur-
d Floyd, the expedition killed its first buffalo. It was a
ill, but the steaks were delicious. They had discovered
)mething that had already been enjoyed by a hundred
enerations of Indians (and would again be "discovered"
· emigrants two generations in the future): the buffalo,
e prairie's grandest feast!

A soldier pointed to a new bird; like millions of
ourists today he had discovered the black and white mag-
e. In August and September they sighted and reported
her "new" animals: the prairie dog, the coyote, the
hite-tailed jackrabbit, and the western grey wolf. They
scovered a new species of deer and called it *mule deer*
ecause of its large ears. And what Captain Clark had at
·st referred to as "beardless goats" they now called *ante-*
be. They found the prickly-pear cactus; it was new and
teresting then, but the next summer they would curse it
ith practiced eloquence.

Gradually experience grew in the minds behind
ose wind-squinted eyes. Notebooks grew thicker, and
e locker of specimens and study skins began to fill. The
en pushed on against the current.

Medicine Creek (South Dakota)

The Tribes of the Seauex Called the Teton, is Camped about 2 Miles up on the N.W. Side, and we Shall Call the River after that Nation, Teton. . . .

WILLIAM CLARK

The late-September days were lovely as they approached the upper Missouri, but the men were nervous. This was the territory of the Teton Sioux. Back in St. Louis frustrated traders had told Captain Lewis about this tribe, who would either block passage of the river completely or demand exorbitant fees to let a trader through. (It made good sense; the Tetons were middlemen in the trading business and knew they would lose profits if St. Louis traders dealt directly with upriver tribes.) And just a month ago the friendly Yankton Sioux had told the captains that the Tetons were raiding their Indian neighbors, too.

The encounter, when it finally came, started innocently enough. On September 23 three Indian boys swam across the river to the strangers' camp. (It's hard to imagine this as anything other than the result of a teen-age dare!) The captains used them as messengers back to their tribe, arranging a council for the next day. That night the boats anchored midstream, with a heavy guard on shore.

The council, on a sandbar, started with standard protocol. The captains presented blankets, coats, and tobacco to their hosts. The Indians' response was standard too: It's not enough; you're cheap; no passage upriver. But here the Tetons encountered a new situation; these men were not ordinary traders. One of the chiefs was insolent with Captain Clark, and the captain responded by drawing his sword. The Indians then drew their bows, and Captain Lewis ordered the soldiers on the boat to prepare to fire. The moment was tense, with cocked weapons and drawn bows. Then twelve more men jumped ashore from the boat, reinforcing the shore guard. The odds now were bad for the Indians, and they withdrew. Things calmed down, but there were many pairs of watchful eyes in the darkness that night.

The next day saw another side of Teton strategy. The captains were carried on painted buffalo robes to a feast and were given full honors: four hundred pounds of excellent buffalo beef, the best parts of roast dog, and pemmican. And entertainment: "10 musitions . . . tambereens . . . sticks with Deer & Goats Hoofs tied so as to make a gingling noise. . . ." But a Mahar prisoner of the Tetons managed to tell one of the soldiers that the Tetons planned to finish off the expedition the next day, so another tense night followed.

When the expedition prepared to leave the following morning there was another face-off. The Indians demanded that the soldiers hand over the cargo and turn around. In answer Captain Clark gave the order to prepare to fire the swivel gun point-blank into the crowd. It was touch and go, but again the Tetons backed down. The river was open.

That night found the expedition miles upriver. The men slept well, but with a heavy guard. Had he known about it, President Jefferson would have slept well too, for this—the first crucial contact in international diplomacy— had succeeded. The new order had challenged the old and had prevailed. The prairie telegraph spread the word of a change in power.

We came [to] and camped . . . about 1/2 a mile below the Ist. Mandin Town. . . . soon after our arrival many men womin & children flocked down to See us, Capt. Lewis walked to the village with the principal Chiefs and our interpters, my Rhumatic complaint increasing I could not go.

WILLIAM CLARK

Two weeks after the encounter with the Teton Sioux, the Corps of Discovery pulled ashore at the Arikara villages. The prairie telegraph had done its work, and the Arikaras knew that these were the men who had faced down the Tetons. At a late-morning council on a day with weather as pleasant as the news, the captains heard the Arikara chief say that "the road was open & no one dare Shut it, & we might Departe at pleasure. . . ."

At this village the expedition realized they had an unexpected resource in Captain Clark's black servant, York. The Indians had never seen a black man and, besides, York was exceptionally strong and intelligent. He roared at the Indian children, who screamed delightedly, and he performed marvelous feats of strength. (York would prove to be a valuable aid in effecting contacts with Indians throughout the whole trip.)

The expedition found that upriver Indian sexual customs, as firm and stern in their own way as the Europeans' in theirs, nevertheless included provisions to pleasure honored guests—and that is just what the soldiers were. Fleeting references in the journals leave no doubt that there is much to be read between the lines.

Autumn was advancing and they had to push on. The cold of the river hurt when they stepped into it now, and some mornings there was ice on the edges. The work and cold water began to tell; three men were hobbled by rheumatism, and once Captain Clark became almost immobile with that ailment in his neck.

But there were blessings: The cold ended the constant harassment by mosquitoes, and the autumn leaves were bright splashes of color against the bluffs and plains. Yellow cottonwood leaves floated down the current to perform stately gavottes in the swirl at the bow of the keelboat, pass under it and disappear. The men saw herds of buffalo swimming from the east bank to the west in their annual trek (and once saw a group of Indians kill more than forty of the vulnerable animals thus engaged). They saw great airborne migrations pass southward by day and heard them by night. It snowed once, and then again. The campfire felt good in the evening, and it felt even better in the morning. The captains issued extra flannel clothing. Now they skinned the animals that had been shot for food, and the men turned out in stiff, rough-tanned capes and coats. It was time to look for winter quarters.

Of help here were the two men, Tabeau and Gravelines, who had temporarily joined the expedition. They were traders who worked this territory and knew the languages. From them the captains learned that the semi-friendly Mandans and their neighbors were being forced northward by the Teton Sioux and had gathered for protection into a large village only a few days ahead. The captains decided to look the situation over when they got there and, if favorable, stop for the winter.

This Morning at Daylight I went down the river with 4 men to look for a proper place to winter proceeded down the river three miles & found a place well Supld. with wood . . . I fell down, and formed a Camp, near where a Small Camp of Indians were hunting. . . .

WILLIAM CLARK

They chose a spot with good wood and game about two miles from the Indian village. There was little time to lose. They set to work at once chopping down trees to build their winter quarters. The shape was triangular—two arms were log rooms, joined at a look-out tower, and the third side, toward the river, was a palisade. There was an outhouse a hundred yards away. They called their building Fort Mandan; they would be here almost six months.

North Dakota winters are never easy, and that of 1804–05 was particularly cold. The temperature stayed below zero for days at a time and once reached forty-five below. Guards (a twenty-four hour watch, of course) had to be changed often in the bitter cold. Hunting became a painful necessity. Hunters were often gone for days at a time, sleeping out on the prairies under fresh-cut skins. Frostbite was common, and once Captain Lewis had to amputate the frozen toes of an Indian boy.

There was plenty of work to do, plenty of firewood to cut. They repaired broken and worn equipment. The two metalsmiths made tools and axeheads out of a damaged sheetmetal stove to trade to the Mandans for corn and potatoes. And there was the scientific work: They cleaned and labeled the specimens they had collected, and packed them to be sent back to St. Louis in the spring. The journals began to fill with details about the Indians' culture—notes that anthropologists still study today.

The captains spent much time with the Indians—Mandans and the various trading parties that came in to barter. These were people who had either been where the expedition was going or knew somebody who knew somebody who had. Translating from lines scratched in the dirt floor with a stick and from gestures indicating waterfalls or mountains or passes or rivers, they began to understand much—and misunderstand some—of what was ahead.

There was diplomacy, too. They tried and even succeeded a little in securing some truces among the constantly raiding plains tribes, telling them that their new white chief in Washington wanted them to live in peace and to be good trading partners. And the Indians weren't the only visitors in camp that winter; there were British traders down from Canada, and the captains told them the astonishing news of the Louisiana Purchase and the change in title to the wilderness.

And there were good times. The journals mention dancing almost every night. Cruzatte had a fiddle, and he somehow kept it from getting smashed or warped or stolen throughout the whole journey. Here, while branches crackled outside in the clear, bitter nights, he played by the roaring fire. The Indians were probably amused at the roughhouse dancing of the soldiers (so crude and simple compared to their own highly developed styles), but York was always a hit. So, while Cruzatte—the son of a French father and a Shawnee mother—played his fiddle and onlookers (dogs and perhaps a horse or two) watched, the Indians, the American soldiers, a black man, some British traders, and others of mixed bloods tried each other's steps. The watch changed and a thankful soldier came in, stomping his feet and blowing on his fingers, to the warmth of a babble of laughter, tall tales, and the exchange of information in a half-dozen languages. The Corps of Discovery was in winter camp.

. . . the men merrily Disposed, I g[a]ve them all a little Taffia and permited 3 Cannon fired, at raising Our flag, Some Men Went out to hunt & the others to Danceing and Continued untill 9 oClock P.M. when the frolick ended &c.

WILLIAM CLARK

"Taffia," a crude, home-brewed rum of limited supply, was usually issued by the captains only on days that had been especially hard or when some difficult task had been accomplished. But today was Christmas, and a celebration was in order. The Indians had been told to stay away from the fort on this occasion, but they knew a "great medicine day" when they saw one, and so they watched anyway.

The most difficult part of this historic journey to reconstruct is the everyday life. Major decisions and events were generally well documented in the journals—but what of the little things (details interesting to us but so commonplace to Lewis and Clark that they never mentioned them)? To find out what life was like at Fort Mandan, we must read between the lines, catching hints wherever we can.

For one thing, it was cold; but this was taken for granted and was not emphasized very much in the journals. When the bitter cold set in—days on end when the temperature didn't even get *up* to zero—the captains sent the men out only occasionally at first, allowing them to get used to it gradually. But there was outdoor work that had to be done. It took an enormous amount of firewood to keep the rooms in the fort warm, besides what was needed to make charcoal for the blacksmith's forge.

The expedition's concept of comfort was completely different from ours today. There is no journal mention of making furniture, so they probably sat on short logs. There was no laundering of the animal-skin clothing, and there were no bedsheets to change. Buffalo hides on a hard floor were warm, but after a while the buffalo hair loosened and stuck to their clothes and got in their eyes. Washing meant warming a pan of water over the fire. And, at forty below, the hundred yards to the unheated outhouse must have seemed like a mile!

The rugged life took its toll in personal injuries and pains. There were bruises from slipping on the ice; fingers sometimes got smashed or twisted. Sergeant Pryor dislocated his shoulder; it took four tries to get it back in place. Occasionally a knife would slip, and twice, at least, men cut themselves seriously with axes. Living around open fires meant frequent burns. Frostbite was common, sometimes severe. And there was rheumatism, especially for Captain Clark. (One day the rheumatism in his neck was so bad he couldn't eat; even so, he spent the day preparing a map.)

It was a typical pioneer winter.

About five Oclock this evening one of the wives of Charbono [Sacajawea] was delivered of a fine boy.

WILLIAM CLARK

During the winter a man named Charbonneau, who was living among the Indians, asked for and received a job as an interpreter for the expedition. (He spoke some Indian languages and French—no English, but a soldier named LaBiche could translate French to English.) He had two Indian wives. One, about sixteen years old, was a Shoshoni (Snake) Indian who had been captured by the Minitaris a few years before and then had been sold or gambled away to Charbonneau. Her name was Sacagawea —a name every modern schoolgirl knows. The captains had now learned enough from the Indians to realize that they would need horses for the overland passage from the headwaters of the Missouri to those of the Columbia and that they would have to buy those horses from Sacagawea's people, the Shoshoni. So when Charbonneau asked to take her along, they agreed.

Buying horses wasn't on anyone's mind on February 11, however. On this day Sacagawea, now just a scared teen-ager, was having a baby, in an earthen Mandan lodge, while snow fell outside. A French trader who happened to be in camp told Captain Lewis that if she drank powdered rattlesnake rattle it might ease the childbirth. They tried it, and the child was born ten minutes later (although Captain Lewis expressed doubt that the potion had helped much). Now this military expedition had both a girl and an infant along!

Spring was coming. The men began preparations early, chopping the pirogues out of the ice and hauling them into the fort for repairs. The navigable part of the river would be narrower from here on, so the keelboat, now too big, was to be sent back to St. Louis with the scientific material gathered so far. A detachment went upstream and found trees big enough to make six dugouts. Now these makeshift sailors had a new craft to master. Their boats would be crude, but they would do.

One day the ice broke in the river, and the men saw an astonishing sight: Bloated carcasses of buffalo that had drowned during the winter and were floating downstream were being retrieved by the Indians—leaping from ice flow to ice flow to get lines around them. There were great feasts of "ripe" buffalo meat, but this was a high-plains delicacy the soldiers were not quite ready for.

On April 7 the keelboat and its crew headed downstream, back to St. Louis. It carried the boxes of hides, Indian artifacts, minerals, pressed plants and study skins, and even some cages with live specimens: a prairie dog, four magpies and a prairie grouse. (The keelboat got back to St. Louis on May 20, and the precious cargo eventually arrived in Washington, to President Jefferson's complete delight and fascination. Parts of its cargo can be seen today at Harvard's Peabody Museum and at the Philadelphia Academy of Natural Sciences.)

Even as the keelboat straightened out in the downstream current, the captains ordered their men into the dugouts and pirogues and headed upstream. They were the final group now, the thirty-three who would go to the coast: twenty-eight soldiers (including the captains), two interpreters, York, Sacagawea, and her infant son. That day Lewis wrote, ". . . we were now about to penetrate a country at least two thousand miles in width: the good or evil it had in store for us was for experiment yet to determine." He was right.

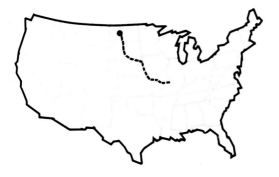

PHOTO BY MIKE SAMPLE

*. . . I determined to encamp on the bank of the Yellow stone river. . . .
the whol face of the country was covered with herds of Buffaloe,
Elk & Antelopes; . . . the buffaloe Elk and Antelope are so gentle
that we pass near them while feeding, without apearing to excite any
alarm among them; and when we attract their attention, they frequently
approach us more nearly to discover what we are. . . .*

MERIWETHER LEWIS

The first day or so out from Fort Mandan the hunters didn't see much game, since animals avoided the large settlement. But it was good to be moving again. Both captains took long walks on shore. On April 9 Clark saw a mosquito—only one, but his memories must have been intense, since he took the trouble to record it in the journal. His apprehension was justified. On the very next day Lewis wrote, "the Muquetoes were very troublesome to us today." And Clark wrote, "the Musquetors troublesom." Apparently the captains sometimes collaborated on their journals, (probably talking as their boats floated side by side); even though their spellings are very different, their phrases are often similar.

Soon game began to appear, in quantities impossible to appreciate today. They saw "emence" herds of bison, elk, deer, and some bear. Beaver began to be plentiful, and it was a delicacy, especially the tail.

Charbonneau, the interpreter they had hired at Fort Mandan, was not a good boatman. Unfortunately he was the one who was steering the pirogue when a sudden gust of wind hit it. He swung the rudder the wrong way, and they were near capsizing when Captain Lewis and Drewyer righted the situation. It could have been disaster. They were two hundred yards out in the swift spring melt, and—because the pirogue was more stable than the dugouts—they had put aboard it the three men who could not swim, Sacagawea and her infant son Jean Baptiste (nicknamed "Pomp" by Captain Clark), and their most valuable papers and trade goods. It was a near thing!

Several times gale-force winds stopped them cold, and they were forced to stay ashore for a day or more. Often the cargo in the dugouts got wet, which meant stopping to dry it. Experience was a good teacher, the only one some of these men had ever had. They learned, and they coped better.

On April 13 they parted company with three white trappers who had tagged along for a while. The Corps of Discovery didn't know it then, but they would not see another "outsider" for almost a year and a half. From here on they would meet only the Americans whose home had been on this continent for millennia.

They began to watch for the mouth of the Yellowstone. During the winter it had been just a charcoal line drawn on deerskin; now they expected any day to round a bend and find it rolling in on their left. When he judged they were close, Captain Lewis walked ahead; he guessed right and found it within ten miles. When the boats came up they celebrated with a dram of whiskey all 'round. Captain Lewis saw that this was an important junction of the western waterways—and thick with beaver besides. He said that a fort should be built here. Twenty-four years later it would be the site of Fort Union (today a national monument).

. . . Capt. Clark killed 2 buffaloe . . . we saved the best meat, and from the cow I killed we saved the necessary materials for making what our wrighthand cook Charbono, calls boudin blanc, *and immediately set him about preparing them for supper; this white pudding we all esteem one of the greatest delicacies of the forrest. . . . About 6 feet of the lower extremity of the large gut of the Buffaloe is the first morsel . . . the mustle lying underneath the shoulder blade next to the back, and fillets are next saught, these are needed up very fine with a portion of kidney suit; to this composition is then added a just proportion of pepper and salt and a small quantity of flour . . . all is compleatly filled with something good to eat, it is tyed at the other end, . . . it is then baptised in the missouri with two dips and a flirt, and bobbed into the kettle; from whence, after it be well boiled it is taken and fried in bears oil until it becomes brown, when it is ready to esswage the pangs of a keen appetite, or such as travelers in the wilderness are seldom at a loss for. . . .*

Meriwether Lewis

The thirty-one healthy men, living outdoors and performing herculean labors as a matter of course, had tremendous appetites. The expedition was usually divided into three "messes," each with its own cook, who was excused from sentry and other duties. A few men who had proved their abilities as hunters, especially Drewyer and Colter, hunted for the whole group. Hunting was easy along this stretch of the upper Missouri; Captain Lewis declared that two men could easily supply a regiment. (This was not merely metaphor; it was a serious consideration for a frontier army—the kind of information the War Department would need to know in case of future operations in the area.)

But this abundance of game could not be counted on for the whole trip, and the cautious captains knew it. Back at the Harper's Ferry armory they had been issued some dried soup with which the army was experimenting (forerunner of the infamous "C-rations"). And during the winter at Fort Mandan they had traded goods to the Indians in exchange for corn. There were some loud minutes now when the captains discovered that some of the men had cut into the reserve corn already. Before the journey's end, a hungry Corps of Discovery would know the taste of poor horse and dog, of tallow candles, and of—nothing.

But this was May and there was plenty of meat. True, spring elk and deer are tough compared to fat autumn ones and, true, the wind blew sand into every bite. But, as Lewis wrote, ". . . our good health and apetites make up every necessary deficiency, and we eat very heartily. . . ."

Bratton . . . . had shot a brown bear which immediately turned on him and pursued him a considerable distance; . . . we at length . . . found him concealed in some very thick brush and shot him through the skull with two balls; . . . we now found that Bratton had shot him through the center of the lungs, notwithstanding which he had pursued him near half a mile; . . . these bear being so hard to die reather intimedates us all; I must confess that I do not like the gentlemen and had reather fight two Indians than one bear. . . .

MERIWETHER LEWIS

Early in May the men found grizzly bear tracks and measured them. They were three times larger than a man's! Back at the Mandan lodges, sprawled around the campfire on winter nights, the soldiers had heard stories from the Indians about these fierce bears. The Indians said that the grizzlies charged instead of retreating; that they were extremely difficult to kill; that before hunting one a man should paint himself just as though he were going to war; and that killing one brought as much honor as "counting coup" (touching) a Blackfoot warrior. And, according to their stories, this was for a good reason; it was not always the grizzly who got killed! But the Corps of Discovery had been issued the prototypes of the brand-new Harper's Ferry 1803 flintlocks, and they were not worried. On April 29 Captain Lewis wrote, "the Indians may well fear this anamal equiped as they generally are with their bows and arrows or indifferent fuzees, but in the hands of skilled riflemen they are by no means as formidable or dangerous as they have been represented."

The first and second grizzlies they shot went down as expected. Maybe their huge size gave the soldiers a slight twinge of uneasiness, but not much more. Then on May 11 Bratton had a run-in with one that refused to die—in fact, it attacked when it should have collapsed. The journal entries began to change their tone.

Three days later they saw one lying in the open, and six hunters crept up on it. From their hiding place forty paces away four of them shot simultaneously, all scoring hits. The old monster attacked. The two who had with-held fire now shot and scored hits too, but these insults merely enraged the bear further. Now it was pandemonium! Men hid behind bushes and went through the complex process of reloading and charging their flintlocks. (Get out powder, measure, and pour into barrel. Get out greased patch and ball, put patch on barrel, put ball on top of it. Draw rammer, ram ball home. Return rammer. Open frizzen. Get out powder again, pour small amount into frizzen pan. Close frizzen. Cock. Fire. Repeat.) But it seemed like each shot had no effect but to announce the hunter's location to the bear, who charged any bush from which a shot came. Two men plunged over a twenty-foot bank into the river; the old bear came right after them. Finally someone put a ball through the bear's head. When they dragged him ashore and butchered him they found he had been hit eight times, including shots through both lungs and a broken shoulder. The matter of how much to respect a grizzly bear was settled beyond argument.

PHOTO BY MIKE SAMPLE

... I beheld the Rocky Mountains for the first time. ... these ... Mountains were covered with snow and the sun shone on it in such manner as to give me the most plain and satisfactory view. while I viewed these mountains I felt a secret pleasure in finding myself so near the head of the heretofore conceived boundless Missouri; but ... I reflected on the difficulties which this snowey barrier would most probably throw in my way to the Pacific, and the sufferings and hardships of myself and party in thim. ...

MERIWETHER LEWIS

Men looked up from their oars to rest a moment and gaze at the Rocky Mountains—snow-capped, distant, silent, huge. The captains paused from writing in their journals to contemplate them. Truth was closing in fast. Only a year before, Jefferson and Lewis and Clark had sat around a map, largely blank, and talked about the intermingling of the headwaters of the Missouri and the Columbia, and of waterborne trade routes from the Orient across the Pacific, up the Columbia, a day's portage across the Divide (made easy with wagons), and down the Missouri to St. Louis and profits. Now, 2300 bone-weary miles from St. Louis, Lewis and Clark were approaching that "day's portage," and hard-won facts were filling in the blanks.

This tough, intelligent, experienced bunch now treated as routine the problems that had licked previous traders and trappers. There were many near-rattlesnake bites, but they killed the snakes and made scientific descriptions of the new species. (They were the first to describe the Northern Pacific rattler and the prairie rattler, but their most exciting new animal in this region was the magnificent bighorn mountain sheep.) They hardly bothered to comment on being chased by grizzlies any more. A pirogue swamped and nearly capsized when Charbonneau once again panicked and did the wrong thing in a squall. Cruzatte (he of the fiddle) cured Charbonneau's panic by threatening to shoot him, and Sacagawea earned the captains' respect by retrieving equipment that floated by. They got ashore and spent two days drying cargo. One night the campfire spread to a tree overhanging the skin tent (copied from the Indians) where the leaders slept. The sentry roused them just in time to escape a large,

burning limb that collapsed where they had been sleeping.

They were expedition-hardened men, who would routinely walk ten miles up a creek just to see what was there. Army-issue woolen clothes and manufactured shoes had disappeared long ago; they wore moccasins and deerskin now, stiff and heavy since there was no time to tan the hides properly. And there was the cold; it was May but they were in the high country. Ice lined the edges of the river in the morning and formed on the oars as they rowed. Worse, they could not row much any more. The Missouri was becoming a mountain river and they had to tow the boats, either wading chest deep in melt water that took their breath away or struggling across jagged rock outcrops. This was the Missouri in spring, eroding a continent to take it to the sea. Dirt banks and overhangs constantly collapsed, and sometimes there were close calls for the dugouts and their crews.

These were not considered remarkable events, recorded with awe or wonder. They were the stuff of every day. And though they didn't know it now, in a few weeks they would look back on these days as the *easy* ones.

... hearing a tremendious roaring above me I ... was ... presented by one of the most beautifull objects in nature, a cascade of about fifty feet perpendicular streching at rightangles across the river from side to side to the distance of at least a quarter of a mile. ... the water decends in one even and uninterupted sheet to the bottom wher dashing against the rocky bottom [it] rises into foaming billows of great hight and rappidly glides away, hising flashing and sparkling as it departs.

MERIWETHER LEWIS

The Great Falls of the Missouri were greeted with relief, and they became both a joy and a misery to the expedition. Two weeks before, the captains had been shocked to find that the river forked; their Indian teachers had given them no hint of such a thing! Which was the true Missouri? (The deceptive fork was actually the Marias River, which at the time they reached the juncture appeared as large as the Missouri because of an unusually heavy spring run-off.) Even after they decided on the south course and had followed it for these two weeks they still were not sure. Now here were the falls, exactly as the Indians had described them—even to a certain eagle's nest.

The falls were a joy because they were beautiful. The mighty Missouri plunged over a series of five falls—the largest almost ninety feet high—with rapids between. Lewis was dumbfounded when he first saw them, resulting in some of the most eloquent writing of the journals. He described it as one of the greatest scenes in the world, and it was. (Niagara was known then, but Victoria Falls and the cataracts of Yosemite and Yellowstone were not.)

And the falls became a misery because the expedition had to portage around them, a portage that lasted eighteen miles. There was no precedent to follow here; all they had to apply to this unforeseeable problem was intelligence and frontier experience. Half the crew cached the pirogues below the portage, since they were too large to be useful farther upstream. Other men found the one large cottonwood in the area and cut four twenty-two-inch wheels from it—not the best wood for this. It was no good at all for axles, so they cut up a pirogue mast for that

purpose. With this man-powered, makeshift wagon they began the long haul around the falls.

This remote spot seemed haunted with strange forces and bad omens. Sacagawea got sick and almost died. Rattlesnakes were common; mosquitoes and gnats were legion. Buffalo came here to drink and to cross the river, and some were swept over the falls. Grizzlies feasted on the carcasses; they had special feelings of territory and were the fiercest the men had encountered. Most of the soldiers were chased at one time or another, some of them twice. Captain Lewis was charged by three buffalo, and he was stalked by a panther-like animal he never did identify.

The portage was long and uphill, and the midsummer heat came down like a weight. The route was thick with prickly-pear cactus that went right through deerskin moccasins, even when they doubled the soles. Men stopped to rest and fell asleep instantly, only to be roused to push on. Rest could wait; summer was passing and the Rockies hadn't even been reached, let alone crossed.

Overleaf: Missouri River (near Craig, Montana)

JUNE 30TH SUNDAY 1805

. . . Men complain of being Soore this day dull and lolling
about. . . . Great numbers of Buffalow in every direction. I think
about 10,000 may be seen in a view.

WILLIAM CLARK

. . . have concluded not to dispatch a canoe with a part of our men to St. Louis as we had intended early in the spring. . . . all appear perfectly to have made up their minds to suceed in the expedition or purish in the attempt. we all beleive that we are now about to enter on the most perilous and difficult part of our voyage, yet I see no one repining; all appear ready to me[e]t those difficulties which await us with resolution and becoming fortitude.

MERIWETHER LEWIS

Independence Day came while the expedition was still struggling around the Falls of the Missouri, so they finished off the whiskey. Their celebration was more than mere formality. Lewis and Clark were both older than the nation. They had been born British citizens before the American Revolution, and Clark's older brother, George Rogers Clark, had played a major role in it. Now they were on a mission of exploration and diplomacy for the young country.

Back in Washington there were fancy-dress balls that night. Perhaps President Jefferson stepped out onto a balcony between dances and looked into the darkness. If he did, his thoughts must have crossed like a silent nightbird across the young nation, passed above the small candle-lit clusters that were Cincinnati and St. Louis, and soared over two thousand miles of dark river to the campfire where Cruzatte played his fiddle and those whose feet were not too sore from cactus spines danced. It was the remotest outpost of empire.

The captains had planned to send a boat back from the falls with scientific specimens and information, as they had from Fort Mandan. Now, with the awesome dimensions of the challenge in front of them becoming clearer, they decided they could not spare the men. (Time would prove them right; they would need all the manpower they had.) So they all celebrated the Fourth facing westward.

The back-breaking portage continued, and the place still seemed strange, out of step. They found a tremendous "fountain," or spring, unlike anything they had ever seen. They heard distant explosions that never were explained.

And here Captain Clark, Charbonneau, Sacagawea, and the infant Pomp had a narrow escape. After seeking refuge in a ravine from a tremendous rain and hailstorm that was bloodying men on the portage, a flash flood suddenly roared down on them. Floundering in water that reached his chest, Clark pushed the Indian girl and her baby up the ravine in front of him. They got out but lost a gun, powderhorn, bullet pouch, and compass in the scramble. The next day they came back and found the compass; they also found a jumble of rocks piled where they had been huddled.

Now they faced a bitter disappointment. Lewis had had the Harper's Ferry armory build a collapsible boat frame that could be covered with hides. They tried it out here, but with no pine pitch to seal the seams the boat failed. They experimented with tallow and sawdust but that didn't work. So they cut two big trees and made two more dugouts instead, abandoning the useless frame.

The work was almost inhumanly hard, but the place was a paradise of game. The captains knew that lean times were coming, so they dried huge amounts of meat and stored the "jerky." On July 15—the falls passed, gear repacked, feet sore—they pushed the overloaded dugouts into the current once again.

The men complain of being much fortiegued. their labour is excessively great. I occasionaly encourage them by assisting in the labour of navigating the canoes, and have learned to push a tolerable good pole *in their [phrase].*

MERIWETHER LEWIS

On a map the Missouri River resembles roughly a large, upside-down fishhook. The long northward course from St. Louis to the Mandan villages is the shank; the stretch across the top of the country from the Mandans to the Great Falls is the curve; and from the falls to its headwaters is the hook. So the men went south now. With the Rocky Mountains towering on their right, sunsets came early. The heat of these summer days sapped their strength, but the chilly nights at this altitude gave at least temporary relief from the mosquitoes and gnats.

But where were the Shoshoni? They should have found them by now; the expedition badly needed guides, and it needed horses even more. The end of their enemy/friend the Missouri was near, and they knew it. Half a season at most and the Rockies would be closed with snow; they must find a route and transportation across them.

Sacagawea had been brought along on the chance she could help establish contact with her people. Now she assured them they were approaching a spot where three rivers came together to become the Missouri; her people would be near there. They hoped she was right.

So the Corps of Discovery went doggedly on. Little of what they had now had been brought from St. Louis. The dugouts had been built along the way. Army-issue clothing had long since given way to buckskins. Axe handles had broken and had been replaced with local wood, then broken and replaced again. The "shoes" on their push poles had broken or pulled off long ago; the jury-rigged replacements were made of spare fishspear points. Luckily, Shields turned out to be an extraordinary backwoods blacksmith and gunsmith; he routinely repaired complex parts and fashioned what they needed from what they had.

More than the equipment was scarred! Sergeant Pryor had dislocated his shoulder lifting a side of buffalo, and it still hurt. York and Charbonneau had stomach problems; maybe it was the alkaline drinking water that most of them were used to by now. Everyone's feet were a complete, painful mess from the sharp rocks and the prickly pear—and they were about to be put afoot. Where were the Shoshoni and their horses?

. . . at the junction of the S.E. fork of the Missouri . . . the country opens suddonly to extensive and beatifull plains and meadows which appear to be surrounded in every direction with distant and lofty mountains; supposing this to be the three forks of the Missouri I halted the party. . . .

MERIWETHER LEWIS

Clark arrived at the three forks of the Missouri first. (They named them the Jefferson, the Madison, and the Gallatin.) He left a note for Lewis and went looking for Shoshoni. On July 26, feet hurting from spine sores and blisters, he walked to the top of a hill twelve miles away. Looked around and walked back, hot and tired. Ate and drank at a spring. Hiked several miles to the Madison. Crossed it (in the process plunging in to rescue non-swimmer Charbonneau from being swept away). Walked four miles looking for Indian sign, not finding any but killing two grizzlies who challenged him on the way. He had high fever and aches that night, so the next day he pressed on only eight miles—and came back twenty to meet Lewis. They decided to stop at this "essential point in the geography of this western part of the Continent" to fix its latitude. Captain Lewis wrote, "intend on taking a tramp myself" to find the Indians. Some tramp!

Look at these remarkable men: the exhausted Clark, sprawled on a buffalo robe, and the perceptive Lewis, on this day carefully describing a new species of black gooseberry in his journal. And especially note three other men: George Drewyer, master hunter; John Colter, green when they started but seasoned hickory now; and John Potts, pleased that a few miles back they'd named a stream for him. "Marked men," historian Bernard DeVoto would call the trio; within five years two would die near this very river junction, and one would become a legend.

In those five years Colter was drawn again and again to the mountains. He wandered awestruck through the wonderland now known as Yellowstone, then rejoined his old expedition companion Potts. And it was back here—near the three forks—that the Blackfeet caught them. They killed Potts but, to amuse the young braves, they stripped Colter and gave him a head start in a game of

pursuit. Colter outran all but one, killed him, plunged into the river he'd helped name the Madison, and hid under some driftwood. When night fell he began to walk, hiding now and then—shivering, alone, and naked. Eight days later he stumbled into Manuel Lisa's new fort on the Bighorn, finding food and relief and a place in America's pantheon of heroes. This was in 1809.

Drewyer heard the tale the next year when he arrived at the fort. He was trapping for Lisa now. Lisa sent him back to the three-forks area, to find a location for a fort he needed from which to tap the beaver wealth first reported here by Lewis and Clark. Drewyer rode in, remembering. A few weeks later the Blackfeet caught him out hunting. He fought like a wild man, but they killed him and took his scalp.

But it was now 1805, and, ignorant of what the future held for them, these men went about the business of setting up camp at the three forks of the Missouri.

The Indian woman [Sacajawea] recognized the point of a high plain to our right which she informed us was not very distant from the summer retreat of her nation on a river beyond the mountains which runs to the west. this hill she says her nation calls the beaver's head from a conceived re[se]mblance of it's figure to the head of that animal. . . . I determined to proceed tomorrow . . . untill I [find] the Indians. . . .

MERIWETHER LEWIS

Finding the Shoshoni was becoming a desperate matter. By all calculations they ought to have met the Indians by now, but still there was no sign of them. In fact, the soldiers had seen no other humans at all since leaving Fort Mandan. They must be in Shoshoni territory by now! Back when they had approached the three forks of the Missouri, Sacagawea had recognized the area and told them the junction was not far off. On reaching the three forks, the expedition had camped on the actual spot where she had been camped with a band of her people when a Minitari war party attacked them and killed several of her people. Sacagawea had fled but was captured four miles up the Jefferson River. She had recognized that spot, too, when they had come to it.

Sacagawea's personality is an interesting puzzle to piece together from the journals. A shimmering romantic legend, far beyond what the record will support, has grown up around her. It has made her a beauty, smiting the hearts of men around her, involving her even in a romance with Clark and crediting her with unerringly guiding the expedition through tangled mountain ranges.

Nonsense. At the crucial points—the Marias River and the three forks—the captains made their decisions based on information they gathered during the winter at Fort Mandan and their own sense of geography, without consulting Sacagawea. As for beauty, there is no reference to her appearance anywhere in the journals. And when they were at the site of her capture, Lewis wrote: ". . . I cannot discover that she shews any immotion of sorrow in recollecting this event, or of joy in being again restored to her native country; if she has enough to eat and a few trinkets to wear I believe she would be perfectly content

anywhere." And as for guiding the expedition through the mountains, consider her age: About seventeen now, she was barely twelve when taken from this region by the Minitaris and then bartered or gambled away to Charbonneau. The legend is just a myth.

But consider again: She apparently had become an accepted, even respected, member of the expedition. There is no reference anywhere to any sense of inconvenience the expedition may have felt from the presence of a female in her teens and her infant, an omission that in itself is significant. And back when the Missouri was a broad torrent that swamped the pirogue and threatened to drown the crew, she had kept her wits about her, grabbing the spilled equipment as it floated by. No word of panic, either, as she scrambled with her baby to escape the flash flood back at the falls. Sacagawea, although not what legend has made her, was nevertheless a remarkable girl.

Now she recognized a rock formation and said that when they saw it from the other side they would be in the summer lands of her people. Lewis decided to take three men ahead on a forced march.

... the road took us to the most distant fountain of the waters of the Mighty Missouri in surch of which we have spent so many toilsome days and wristless nights. ... two miles below McNeal had exultingly stood with a foot on each side of this little rivulet and thanked his god that he had lived to bestride the mighty & heretofore deemed endless Missouri. ... I now descended the mountain about 3/4 of a mile which I found much steeper than on the opposite side, to a handsome bold runing Creek of cold Clear water. here I first tasted the water of the great Columbia river.

MERIWETHER LEWIS

When they left the three forks, the expedition headed up the brush-choked rapids of the Jefferson River, straight into the Rockies. It was the two-rope constantly now. Hours of wading made feet tender; then the rocks sliced them. The expedition was on the thin edge of exhaustion and disaster.

August 6 was a typical day. Lewis and three men had gone ahead, and on this day the two parts of the expedition almost lost touch when a beaver expropriated the green willow stick which held a note Lewis had left for Clark. Drewyer, out hunting, found Clark's group and the two groups reestablished contact. A dugout swung in a rapids; Whitehouse was thrown out and the boat rolled over him. (Though in bad shape for days he recovered okay, but Lewis declared that two inches less water and Whitehouse would have been killed.) Later the same day two other dugouts also swamped. Some of the cargo was lost or damaged irreparably, and all of it was wet. That night a panther took three deerskins they had placed in a tree. A hunter, Shannon, failed to return from a hunt. (He would walk in several days later, having subsisted off the land—the result of experience; a year before when lost he had nearly starved in the midst of plenty.) Clark's ankle was still sore and painful from a boil and the cactus spines. The journals say "proceeded on with much dificuelty and fatigue over rapids & Stones." And finally there was the weather report: "this evening a violent wind from the N.W. accompanied with rain."

Where were the Shoshoni? Some tracks Clark found suggested that maybe the Indians had already seen the soldiers or heard their guns and were avoiding them. Did the Shoshoni think the soldiers were Blackfeet? The captains instructed the men to leave bits of paper and cloth about to show that they were white men and not Blackfeet. (There is irony in this; the Shoshoni had never *seen* white men!)

Putting their faith in Sacagawea's belief that her people were just over the pass, Captain Lewis and his three men kept pushing ahead.

It really was not far. The Jefferson dwindled to a trickle, and they had a moment of triumph over the "hitherto endless" Missouri. Then over Lemhi Pass, and they found a spring—whose water flowed west! That meant it was a stream that traveled to a river, perhaps one or two more rivers, and then to the Columbia and the Pacific. The first white men were across the Continental Divide!

. . . we met a party of about 60 warriors mounted on excellent horses who came in nearly full speed. . . . the chief and two others who were a little in advance of the main body spoke to the women, and they informed them who we were and exultingly shewed the presents which had been given them. these men then advanced and embraced me very affectionately. . . . bothe parties now advanced and we wer all carresed and besmeared with their grease and paint till I was heartily tired of the national hug. I now had the pipe lit and gave them smoke. . . .

MERIWETHER LEWIS

While still crossing the Divide, Captain Lewis and his three men saw one Indian, alone. Unfortunately Lewis had deployed his men far out to either side (they had lost the trail and were looking for it), and the Indian must have thought they were trying to surround him. He fled.

The next day they went down the west side of the Divide. (It is astonishing, and it happens over and over: On days as crucial as this one Lewis takes time to make close botanical descriptions of new shrubs and grasses.) At mid-morning they saw a man, two women, and some dogs. The people ran. Lewis tried to tie some gifts to the dogs, but they ran away too.

They followed the trail the three people had taken. Within a mile they turned a corner and suddenly came upon two Indian girls and an old woman. One of the girls fled, but the others, seeing no chance to escape, sat and bowed their heads to accept their fate as captives. Lewis realized that he and his trail-worn men were hardly distinguishable from Indians, so he pulled up his sleeve to show his white skin. A wonder! And he gave them gifts: "some beads a few mockerson awls some pewter looking glasses and a little paint." It was extravagant, but this was not a moment to be conservative. Drewyer was fluent in the sign language, and he asked the old woman to call the girl who had run off; Lewis feared she would alarm the tribe. She came back and received gifts too. Then Lewis painted the cheeks of both girls with vermillion, since Sacagawea had told him this was a sign of peace among the Shoshoni. When the women calmed down after this meeting—a meeting that was to live in the history of the tribe as an epic event—the explorers asked to be taken to the Indian camp.

They had gone about two miles when they heard pounding hoofbeats, and sixty warriors came toward them at full speed. (The first Indians they had seen that morning had carried the alarm to the village.) Captain Lewis left his gun and advanced with the flag, but the chief was more interested in what the women were saying. Lewis' generosity now paid off as the women told the chief that these strangers were something unprecedented—men with white skins, and generous, too! Tension turned to gaiety as the parties whooped it up and got acquainted. The chief's name was Cameahwait; later the soldiers would realize how fateful a coincidence it was that he was the one they had met.

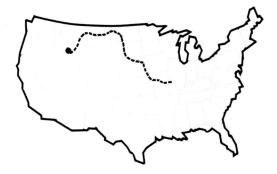

... Capt. Clark arrived with the Interpreter Charbono, and the Indian woman [Sacajawea], who proved to be a sister of the Chief Cameahwait. the meeting of those people was really affecting. ... we had the satisfaction ... to find ourselves ... with a flattering prospect of being able to obtain as many horses shortly as would enable us to prosicute our voyage by land should that by water be deemed unadvisable.

MERIWETHER LEWIS

Captain Lewis and his small advance party stayed two nights with Cameahwait's band. These Indians did not have an easy existence. Their fear of the Blackfeet down in the area Lewis and Clark had just come through kept them in the high country, where there were no buffalo, the source of every good thing. The first day, Lewis saw twenty Indians chase ten antelope for two hours without getting one—an object lesson: With primitive weapons it took extreme effort to get even a little bit to eat. The soldiers must have felt renewed pride in their modern guns.

At one meal Captain Lewis was given a piece of salmon, and by this knew for a certainty that these waters led to the Pacific. And there was another encouragement, indeed a vast relief—the horse herd. There were horses of every size and every description, almost 700 of them. Eighteenth-century men were as familiar with horses as later men would be with cars, and to these long-afoot soldiers it must have seemed like payday. It was good to be around horses again, Lewis thought; their sounds and smells were comforting to go to sleep to.

Lewis tried at once to get Cameahwait to go back with him to meet Clark and the rest of the men, who were still struggling up the other side of the Divide. With sudden changeableness the Indians became suspicious. Was this man with the gifts leading them into a Blackfoot ambush? Lewis was superb. He spoke with respect and challenge, request and sarcasm, blending them in perfect proportions. He promised the Indians they would receive marvelous gifts and would see a black man! (These Indians had seen only Indians before. Lewis was the first sight of the white man. Were there black men in the world too?) And Lewis said there was even a girl who spoke their language. Besides, were they cowards? He persuaded and prodded them, and they went.

But he had to keep persuading them as they worked their way back over the pass. The touchiest moment came when they got back to the spot where Lewis had left a note for Clark (on a *dry* stick, he specifies—one a beaver wouldn't want). The note was there but no Clark; he had not come up yet. Something akin to panic set in with the Indians, now certain they had been tricked. In a desperate final effort to convince them they were not expecting ambush, the soldiers gave their rifles to the Indians and put Indian garments on themselves. It worked; the Indians agreed to wait for a short time.

How to tell the next part? Are there fairy tales in history books? Do hidden fingers weave the separated strands of history so they again mesh? Clark and the rest appeared on the scene, and in the tumult Lewis called Sacagawea out to translate. She started; she hesitated; and the astonishing coincidence was revealed: Cameahwait was her brother! These white men had returned her to the very band from whom she had been stolen.

In his journal, Lewis does not dwell too much on this reunion, but he must have realized that this happy coincidence greatly improved the chances of getting horses from the Shoshoni.

I . . . asked Cameahwait by what rout the Pierced nosed indians
[Nez Perce], who . . . inhabited this river below the mountains,
came over to the Missouri; this he informed me was to the north,
but added that the road was a very bad one. . . . however knowing that
Indians had passed, and did pass, at this season on that side of
this river to the same below the mountains, my rout was instantly
settled in my own mind. . . .

MERIWETHER LEWIS

A sense of climax pervades the meeting with the Shoshoni. There was the drama of Sacagawea discovering her brother, but there was more. For five months now the expedition had been crossing the plains; they had been waterborne; and in all this time they had not seen any other people. Now the plains were finished; the dugouts were weighted with stones and sunk; and the expedition was in camp with Indians. For a few hours the men relaxed and enjoyed a sense of what they had accomplished.

The feeling could not last. Far though as they had come, they had barely penetrated the Rocky Mountains. And although they could not know it, this was about the worst place they could have chosen to try to cross the mountains. It was late August, and the high country had snow. They needed to discover a route or be taught one, for they must push on.

The captains decided to split again. Lewis would stay with the Shoshoni to make preparations for the next push while Clark would take eleven men and go on ahead to scout out a route.

Should Clark's group go down the Lemhi River, which was just across the Divide? It had enough water to float the boats and it must get to the Pacific eventually. There was an old Indian in Cameahwait's band they called Toby. He had never gone down the river—nobody had—but years before he had crossed the mountains on a land trail quite a way north, and the Indians on the other side (first mention of the Nez Perce) had told him the river route was impossible because of rapids and falls. Clark decided to check it out.

The Lemhi was traversable and soon joined the Salmon. The scouting party passed two Indian fishing camps and stopped each time to buy some fish, because one of the problems of this high country was becoming clear: There was not enough game to supply the expedition. This wasn't the only problem. The banks—if you could call them that (really they were just mountains coming straight down into the water)—got worse and worse the farther downstream the men scrambled. The conclusion was becoming obvious, but Clark took four men and went twenty miles more just to make sure. He probably entered the mountain-walled, rapids-choked section that even today is called "The River of No Return" and was convinced. This route was impossible. There were no trees big enough to make dugouts; the rapids were impassible; the rockslide slopes were too dangerous for man or horse (Clark slipped once and hurt his hip badly); and game was too scarce to feed the company.

This should not be considered a defeat. It was a route check, a necessary increment for intelligent decision-making. The two captains pooled what they had learned, Clark from his reconnaissance and Lewis from questioning the Shoshoni. They decided they must find the overland route to the north that they had heard about. Toby agreed to go along as their guide.

. . . we . . . proceded on thro' thickets in which we were obliged to Cut a road, over rockey hill Sides where our horses were in [per]peteal danger of Slipping to their certain distruction & up & Down Steep hills, where Several horses fell, Some turned over, and others Sliped down Steep hill Sides, one horse Crippeled & 2 gave out.

WILLIAM CLARK

The decision to go north and find the land route across the Bitterroots, instead of attempting to descend the Salmon River, meant that the Corps of Discovery would proceed on foot or, if possible, mounted. They bartered with the Shoshoni for horses but it was not easy. The Indians were about to make their annual trip down to the buffalo plains, the need for winter meat overcoming their fear of the Blackfeet. They would need their horses. The captains were forced to dig deep into their dwindling supply of trade goods, and even firearms; Clark gave up a pistol with a hundred balls, and powder, and a knife—all for one horse. The knife was probably one made from the damaged stove at Fort Mandan, but he was not eager to give up the pistol. Even going to these lengths they got just twenty-nine horses, not the best. Clark wrote of these animals that there were "Several Pore, & young. [The] horses are indifferent, maney Sore backs and others not acustomed to pack. . . ." The soldiers would have to walk; the horses would carry supplies. The men made sacks out of hides, transferred their gear from boxes to the sacks, and used the wood from the boxes to make pack saddles.

Then they headed north, with the abrupt ramparts of the Bitterroots on their left. They followed the Salmon River—until it turned left and headed straight through the mountains, cutting the awesome canyon that Clark had scouted and now described to the men. They left the Salmon, kept on northward and began to climb.

This was to be their first experience in rugged, high-mountain travel and—frontiersmen though they were—nothing in their experience had prepared them for it. These were the Rocky Mountains, young and sharp—not the ancient, rolling Alleghenies. The men climbed on talus, whole mountainsides of piled rock without plants or

even soil. The weather turned bad. Phrases from Clark's journal tell of their discomfort and struggles: ". . . rain . . . in the evening . . . obliges us to Continue all night. . . . Some of the worst roads that ever horses passed . . . snow about 2 inches deep [and] rain which termonated in a Sleet . . . a verry cold morning every thing wet and frosed, we detained untill 8 oClock to thaw the covering for the baggage &c &c." It was hard on men and horses and equipment. Their last thermometer got broken; it was a severe loss considering the scientific purposes of the expedition.

But they made it. The main range of the Bitterroots was still on their left—they had crossed over an eastward leg of it and were now descending into a long, beautiful, north-trending valley. It had been an enlightening prologue for the main crossing.

... we met a part[y] of the Tushepau [Flathead] nation, of 33 Lodges about 80 men 400 Total and at least 500 horses, those people recved us friendly, threw white robes over our Sholders & Smoked in the pipes of peace. ... I was the first white man who ever wer on the waters of this river.

WILLIAM CLARK

When the expedition came down into the valley of the Bitterroot River, they met a band of the Tushepau nation. For some reason we do not know they began calling these Indians "Flatheads," and the name stuck. (They did not have flat heads.)

The band was a large one, about four hundred people in thirty-three lodges. Their existence was similar to that of the Snake Indians. Most of the year they lived in the high country, kept there by fear of the Blackfeet down on the prairies. When it was time to stock up for winter, they made a fast, nervous trip down to the prairies to hunt buffalo. For this they needed horses, and in horses they were rich. Clark counted at least five hundred and immediately began to bargain for some.

The bargaining was not easy. These Indians had a gutteral language—Clark called it "gugling"—unlike any other the expedition had encountered. Luckily there was living among the Flatheads a Shoshoni boy who spoke both Flathead and Shoshoni. The bargaining went like this: Clark would make an offer in English. Private La-Biche translated it to French. Charbonneau translated from French to Minitari. His wife Sacagawea changed the French to Shoshoni, which the boy rendered in Flathead! Somehow it worked, and the expedition bought thirteen horses and exchanged seven of their worn-out animals for fresh ones. Three of the new animals were colts which could not carry full loads but would make better eating when lean times came.

The visit was not long. The Flatheads were anxious to start for the three forks of the Missouri for their annual buffalo hunt, and the Corps of Discovery were still racing winter. Much better mounted now, the Corps headed on up the valley. It was good traveling compared to what they had just experienced (and it was heaven compared to what was coming). There were small problems—at first they had to post a watch over their new horses to keep them from going back to the Flatheads—but they averaged about twenty miles a day.

(There was a flurry of excitement when three Flatheads rode in hellbent for leather after two Snakes who had stolen twenty Flathead horses. True, the Snakes were neighbors; in fact, the Flatheads were going to join the Snakes, who also feared the Blackfeet, for the buffalo hunt. But horses were horses, and honor was honor. The braves wolfed down some boiled venison and dashed away on their quest.)

A creek came in from the left, out of the mountains, and old Toby recognized it. Here was where they should turn and force the Bitterroots. Time was short—there was snow everywhere now, not just up on the peaks—and they were tempted to start up the creek at once. But this trail was high, freezing, rough, and barren—an agony, as their information from the Snakes and the Flatheads had warned. So they stayed here at the junction an extra day, naming the camp "Traveler's Rest." They grazed the horses, hunted for meat, and rested. The expedition was about to face its greatest challenge.

SEPTEMBER 14TH THURSDAY 1805

*We . . . Encamped opposit a Small Island at the mouth of a branch
on the right side of the river, . . . here we were compelled to
kill a Colt for our men & Selves to eat for the want of meat & we named
the South fork Colt killed Creek, and this river we Call Flat head River. . . .*

WILLIAM CLARK

The expedition wanted to leave Traveler's Rest on the morning of September 11, but during the night two of the horses had strayed. The men finally found them, but they didn't get started until three o'clock. The going wasn't bad but they saw no game; at this rate the four deer they had been able to shoot at Traveler's Rest were not going to last the thirty-three people very long. They made seven miles and camped.

The day of September 12 was harder. They found the steep mountainside very bad—"intolerable," Clark said, and he was a man who had seen some—but following the creekbed instead meant hacking their way through a jackstraw jumble of fallen timber and brush. They crossed a mountain—eight miles without water. Clark found some pine trees with the bark peeled, and Sacagawea told him that Indians using this trail had done this to get at the inner bark for food. It made sense; the day's success in hunting had totaled one pheasant. The rear marchers came into camp at ten o'clock, "party and horses much fatigued."

The next morning the horses had strayed again. (This matter of the horses straying was not just carelessness. They could have hobbled them but it was more important that the animals get a chance to forage.) They finally got started and just a few miles out found an astonishing thing —a hot spring. There was even a place hollowed out by Indians for a bathtub. Only the urgent press of time kept them from the luxury of a hot bath in the wilderness. They passed beaver dams but the hungry men saw no beaver. Clark again notes that the "road" is intolerable, only this time adds "as usial."

The fourteenth was hard going. Clark wrote that it "fatigues our men and horses" again, and then added "exceedingly." This from a man who measured with a pioneer's scale of fatigue. They left the ridge and picked

and scrambled their way down a faint trail to the creek in the ravine, Toby in the lead. It had been many years since the old Indian had made his trip over this trail, and here he made a mistake. He left the main trail on the ridge and followed a side trail down to an Indian fishing camp. They found a brush fish-trap, but no fish. They were out of food and agreed to kill a colt. It was their first meal of horsemeat; there would be more.

The fifteenth started with horsemeat for breakfast, then became a day of aching muscles, gasping lungs, and sharp side aches. The exertion was awful, and still they made only twelve miles, climbing back out of the ravine and up to the ridge over a way the journal calls "as bad as it can possibly be to pass." (Indian trails typically followed the ridges, whereas later white-man roads would follow the valleys.) Two horses gave out. One horse slipped and rolled forty yards down the mountain, smashing Clark's field desk which held the expedition's notes. There was a scramble to retrieve the precious papers.

Evening camp was welcome. The men melted snow for water, finished off the last of the colt, rolled up in their tattered blankets or buffalo robes, and wondered what more the next day could bring!

I . . . decended the mountain to a leavel pine Countrey proceeded on through a butifull Countrey for three miles to a Small Plain in which I found maney Indian lodges. . . . They call themselves Cho pun-nish *or* Pierced noses *[Nez Perce].*

WILLIAM CLARK

Misery joined the expedition on September 20. At sunup the snow was four inches and still falling. The men mended moccasins and wrapped cloth or hides around their feet for socks. Clark saw a deer, but his flintlock misfired seven times, and they left hungry. The trail was a repetition of yesterday's nightmare, but now snow hid the already treacherous footing, and men and horses fell constantly. A cloud settled on the ridge, cutting visibility and bringing with it a damp, penetrating cold. "I have been wet and as cold in every part as I ever was in my life," Clark wrote. They killed another colt for supper and camped where it was scarcely level enough to lie down. The next day was more of the same; that night they killed the last colt and rolled up in wet blankets.

It was a crisis. The incredible exertions were taking their toll. Morale was down and something akin to despair was settling in. All they could see in any direction was more of these tangled, rugged mountains. It was magnificent scenery, but nobody noticed. Had this cursed trail no end? The captains decided that Clark would push ahead with six of the strongest men—to find food and a way down from the high country.

Captain Clark left at dawn. His party's effort is incredible to ponder, but it paid off. In twenty miles they reached a peak where at last they could see a low plain, far to the southwest. So there *was* an end to it! They pushed on twelve more miles and camped, supperless, naming their campsite "Hungry Creek." Captain Lewis' men may have had it better, but not much. They made eighteen miles and dined on tallow candles.

September 29 was another day of hellish winter travel for Clark's men, but they found and killed a stray Indian horse. They ate part and strung the rest up for the others. Unfortunately, Lewis' group didn't get that far that day and camped cold, wet, and still hungry. Next day at midmorning they found the horse carcass and tore at it gratefully; but camp, ten hours later, was again cold. This was the eighth day of this awful passage, and for Lewis' group the end was not even in sight. It is incredible that on this day Lewis' journal opens with a description of a new bird, makes some geological observations, and closes with notes on a new kind of honeysuckle!

But the end of hell was near. Clark's group came down a ridge and into a Nez Perce Indian encampment.

The Cho-pun-nish or Pierced nose Indians are Stout likely men, handsom women, and verry dressey in their way, the dress of the men are a White Buffalow robe or Elk Skin dressed with Beeds which are generally white, Sea Shells & the Mother of Pirl hung to ther hair & on a piece of otter skin about their necks, hair Ceewed in two parsels hanging forward over their Sholders, feathers, and different Coloured Paints which they find in their Countrey Generally white, Green & light Blue. Some fiew were a Shirt of Dressed Skins and long legins & Mockersons Painted. . . .

WILLIAM CLARK

The Nez Perce diet consisted mostly of the tuberous camas root and salmon from the great runs that still came up the rivers then. The starving soldiers gorged themselves on this great but unfamiliar feast. Captain Clark purchased as much as a horse could carry and sent Reuben Field to take it back to Lewis and his men, whose only food had been a coyote Lewis had shot and some crayfish the men had picked from a stream. Field appeared to them like a saint; they ate and then stumbled on down to the Nez Perce camp, their ordeal over.

But now they faced new problems. Something, probably the radical change in diet, nearly incapacitated the Corps of Discovery. Men got off their horses and lay by the trail, vomiting and diarrhetic. Lewis could scarcely move for one whole day. The Nez Perce were helpful and the captains administered what medicines they could, but it took time for their bodies to adjust to the new food. They tried to restore meat to their diet and managed to shoot a few deer. They also began to eat dog, which from now on would be one of their staples—until they returned to the buffalo plains a year later. (Dog meat was much to Clark's distaste; he was the only one who never did develop a tolerance for it. Most of the soldiers grew to even relish it.)

The expedition moved to a place on the Clearwater River where some large ponderosa pines were available for making dugouts, and those who were well enough set to work. Sick and short-handed, this time they used the slower, easier Indian method—using fire rather than chisels to hollow out the logs. By October 6 they finished five dugouts. One night they secretly buried some goods to be retrieved on the return trip. The invaluable Shields made a branding iron and they branded their horses. The Nez Perce promised to care for the herd until the expedition returned. (The tribe would keep their promise. In fact, when a flood exposed the secret cache, the Nez Perce rescued the hidden goods and held them for the soldiers' return!) The Corps of Discovery was about to become waterborne again.

The captains were still feeling the effects of sickness, and their journals do not express the jubilation they must have felt when, on October 7, they put the tiny flotilla into the swift current of the Clearwater. For the first time on the whole trip, they would be going *with* the current!

. . .towards evening we met Several Indians in a canoe who were going up the River. they Signed to us that in two Sleeps we Should See the Ocean. . . .

JOSEPH WHITEHOUSE

They were going downstream but it was no holiday! True, there was exhilaration in the swift motion and the way the rocks glided by so effortlessly, but their course now was on fast, rocky rivers. The first day a dugout rammed a rock and split. The water happened to be shallow and nobody drowned, but it made the men realize that going down the Clearwater would not be like going up the Missouri! So the resilient Corps of Discovery developed the skills they needed. They learned how to read rapids from above—when to portage and when to dare. They still upset, often; it was a wild river. So they packed drier and distributed the load better.

They reached the Snake and rushed on to the Columbia. At that important juncture they stopped to take sightings and fix its location. Then it was downstream with the great Columbia, salmon from the ocean glowing ghostlike in the clear depths and the silhouette of the Cascade Range slowly changing as the river turned, straightened, and turned again, carrying the expedition closer to its goal.

Anxious to reach the sea, the men ran rapids they might otherwise have portaged. Still, some were impossible, so they packed the cargo around them and let the dugouts down with lines. At others, a bit less awesome, the non-swimmers walked while the swimmers took the boats through, yelling and laughing for the pure energy of it. At one place the whole river was forced to a width of only forty-five yards, between gate-like cliffs that made portage impossible. Clark wrote, "I deturmined to pass through this place notwithstanding the horrid appearance of this agitated gut swelling, boiling & whorling in every direction." The Indians gathered on the cliffs to watch the disaster—and were astonished to see the tiny boats shoot out safely on the smoother waters below.

The expedition has been helped, even saved, by Indians time after time. The Indians along here, however, were a disappointment to the expedition—beggars and thieves who pilfered whatever took their fancy. But they made magnificent canoes—in which they nonchalantly negotiated tremendous winds and waves. Of great interest to the expedition, too, were the pieces of metal and cloth the Indians had in their possession—trinkets that could only have come from ship's traders at the Columbia's mouth. And occasionally they startled the soldiers with a familiar word, used like nonsense but unmistakeably English!

Events were piling into one another now. Memories that included the slow Missouri, the Mandan winter, the endless herds of buffalo, the meeting with Cameahwait, and the awful crossing of the Rockies now strained to round one more bend. . .

Overleaf: Pacific Ocean from the mouth of the Columbia River

NOVEMBER 7TH THURSDAY 1805

*Great joy in camp we are in view of the Ocian . . . this great
Pacific Octean which we been so long anxious to See. and the
roreing or noise made by the waves brakeing on the rockey Shores
(as I suppose) may be heard disti[n]ctly.*

MERIWETHER LEWIS

Epilogue

They were on the coast. Americans had succeeded in crossing the continent! And now they were wintering by the Pacific Ocean. It was a dreary, grey winter; it rained almost every day. But the food was adequate so it was not hardship. They boiled seawater to get salt for the return journey, hunted, made moccasins. Once they made a short trip to see a whale that had been washed ashore. Sacagawea went along. (What tales this mountain Indian girl was accumulating!)

In the spring they began the trip back. It was another epic journey, and the journals make absorbing reading. Part of the time they split into groups to make side explorations. On one of these Captain Lewis had a run-in with the Blackfeet and killed two of them, barely escaping himself. There were the usual hardships, encounters with grizzly bears, and boat accidents—and a near disaster when Cruzatte accidentally shot and wounded Lewis. But they made it, and in September, 1806—worn, battered, experienced, excited—they came floating down to a tumultuous welcome in St. Louis.

The first results of the expedition came immediately. From tavern to shop to cabin the word spread of the incredibly rich fur country they had found, and the next spring a steady stream of trappers headed up the Missouri. The stream became a flood that did not end until changing fashions killed the fur trade in the 1840s.

Another result of the journey was a negative. The old dream of a northwest passage—a water route to India—was laid to rest. It was obvious now that no one could make a profit on commerce that involved a land passage over the Rockies, and the water route simply did not exist. Instead, the expedition had found a rich new land one that would make men finally stop thinking about India.

And they had brought that rich land into the orbit of the United States. This was the supreme and lasting contribution of the Lewis and Clark Expedition. It was *Americans,* not representatives of any European powers, who first crossed the continent in temperate regions and established a claim on the Upper Missouri, the Rockies, and the Columbia-drained Pacific Northwest. This did not become fact all at once, but when it did, it was because of the vision of Thomas Jefferson and the courageous determination of the men of the Lewis and Clark Expedition. Dugouts do not ordinarily leave marks, but theirs did. They left the tracks of empire.

There is still another—perhaps more rewarding—way of looking at the crossing; it is to look at the experience of the men who did it. Nations rise and merge, political allegiances change; but these men lived an experience that is theirs alone. We think of them now Captain Meriwether Lewis, magnificent on the journey but who would die, murdered or a suicide, just a few years later; Captain William Clark, who would live a long and rewarding life as Indian agent and Grand Old Man in St. Louis; Shannon, who would become a senator in Kentucky; Gass, Willard, and Bratton, who would live to see men cross the continent on iron rails; Colter, Droulliard, and others who would go back to the mountains and streams they had named; Sacagawea and Charbonneau, who would return to live with the Indians of the middle Missouri, and their son "Pomp," who would spend some time with Clark, travel to Europe, receive an education, and then become a mountain man; the black man York, who would be freed by Clark after the journey. (Some evidence has him doing poorly in a freight-hauling business in Tennessee; other evidence has him returning to the Indians among whom he had known glory and living with them in respect and honor. If the latter is not true, it should have been.)

To the end of their days there was a bond of experience among them that even Thomas Jefferson, whose eyes ached for the West, could not share. These men had crossed mountains that had no highways, floated rivers that had no dams, seen buffalo that had no limit, talked with Indians that had no masters. They were the first.

The expedition of Messrs. Lewis and Clarke, for exploring the river Missouri, and the best communication from that to the Pacific Ocean, has had all the success which could have been expected. They have traced the Missouri nearly to its source, descended the Columbia to the Pacific Ocean, ascertaining with accuracy the geography of that interesting communication across our continent, learned the character of the country, of its commerce, and inhabitants; and it is but justice to say that Messrs. Lewis and Clarke, and their brave companions, have by this arduous service deserved well of their country.

—Thomas Jefferson, in his message
to Congress, December 2, 1806

Meriwether Lewis   William Clark

Books in the "Voyage of Discovery" series: California Trail, Lewis & Clark, Mormon Trail, Oregon Trail, John Wesley Powell, Santa Fe Trail.
Also available is a book on the Oregon Trail Center near Baker City, Oregon.
Selected titles in this series can be ordered with a booklet in German or Spanish bound into the center of the English book.

Call (800-626-9673), fax (702-433-3420), write to the address below,
Or visit our website at www.kcpublications.com

Published by KC Publications, 3245 E. Patrick Ln., Suite A, Las Vegas, NV 89120.

Created, Designed, and Published in the U.S.A.
Printed by Doosan Dong-A Co., Ltd., Seoul, Korea
Color Separations by Kedia/Kwang Yang Sa Co., Ltd.
Paper produced exclusively by Hankuk Paper Mfg. Co., Ltd.